EMERALD WATERS
OF THE ROCKIES

THE REALM OF WILD, PRISTINE BEAUTY

Photographs and text by
GEORGE BRYBYCIN

❄❄❄❄❄❄❄❄❄❄ G B PUBLISHING ❄❄❄❄❄❄❄❄❄❄

Photographic studies by George Brybycin:

The High Rockies
Colourful Calgary
Our Fragile Wilderness
The Rocky Mountains
Banff National Park
Jasper National Park
Colourful Calgary II
Wildlife in the Rockies
Rocky Mountain Symphony
Enchanted Wilderness
Wilderness Odyssey
Rocky Mountain Symphony II
Romance of the Rockies
Calgary - The Sunshine City
The Living Rockies
Cosmopolitan Calgary
Banff and Jasper N.P.
The Rockies: Wildlife
The Majestic Rockies
Emerald Waters of the Rockies
The Canadian Rockies Panoramas

Text Editor: Sheldon Wiebe
Design: George Brybycin
Printed and bound in Singapore by
Kim Hup Lee Printing Co Pte Limited

ISBN 0-919029-22-1 Paperback

For current list, please write to:

GB PUBLISHING, Box 6292, Station D,
Calgary, Alberta Canada T2P 2C9

If you love this still beautiful planet and all of its many wonders (including humanity), then adapt these simple ideas for your lifestyle:

- Respect and protect nature and our environment.
- Educate your family and friends about environmental issues.
- Support environmental organizations - buy memberships.
- Plant a tree, or two or ten, in your yard and have your own miniature forest with birds and squirrels, and all the nature sights, sounds and smells they bring.
- Remember that one tree absorbs 4.5 kilograms of carbon monoxide per year. Hug a tree, it cleans the air you breathe - it is your friend.
- If a tree is exposed to 20 kilograms of pollutants a year, it will sicken and die (in just the same way that people exposed to radiation sicken and die).
- When you hike in the wilderness - pack your trash out.
- Admire the intricate beauty of a wild flower, but never pick it - flowers must mature in order to produce seeds and reproduce.
- In areas where there are sidewalks - use them! Grass breathes carbon dioxide and produces oxygen. Do not destroy it.
- Hunt only if you need the meat for food. Too many species have become endangered as a result of hunting for pleasure.
- Buy a synthetic Christmas tree and use it for thirty years. If we all did this, think of the real trees we could save.
- Recycle. Recycle. Recycle. Use both sides of all paper; use the same shopping bag until it begins to wear out (then use it as a garbage bag); return all deposit products for refunds. Every little bit helps.
- Overly packaged, or disposable products create non-biodegradable landfill. Avoid them at all costs.
- Buy carefully. More and more environmentally friendly products are available all the time. Use them.
- Think before you do... Make the environmentally wise decision.
- Rid yourself of greed and materialism.
- Vote for political candidates who run "green" campaigns. And if they get elected, hold them to their "green" campaign promises.
- Avoid smoking. Not only does it cause cancer, but it deadens the senses and shortens the breath. And the smells of nature are not to be missed.
- Drink less today than you did yesterday. Drinking alcohol kills brain cells and deadens the senses.
- Drugs? Drugs are deceptive, extremely addictive, they kill the will and deaden the senses (do you sense a trend here)?
- Be kind, friendly and gentle. Compassion and kindness are never embarrassing, even for professional athletes.

Remember, we will all continue to be healthy and alive only as long as we help Mother Nature to be the same.
I ask that you will understand what I am saying.
Will you? Please?

WESTWARD HO, 1994!
The Adventures of Chiori, Helga and Lynn

July 11/94

Helga and Chiori were waiting for me when I arrived in Calgary shortly after 9:00 a.m. MDT. They had driven in from Winnipeg and arrived the previous evening.

We went along to downtown Calgary to see what events were taking place. We saw Indians on horseback, a marching band, square dancing on the street and visited a RCMP mobile museum on our way to Rope Square (known as Olympic Square the rest of the year). People were extremely helpful and friendly. The whole city seemed to be in western dress, welcoming all with "Ya hoo", the official greeting of theStampede.

We went to Carol and Doug's for lunch - getting only a bit lost on the way. There we were heartily welcomed and joined cousins Jim and Rae Thomson from the Toledo area at the "Fraser Campground". Cousin Gordy dropped in, so we had a "photo op".

Helga knew that Sun Ice had an outlet so we went there before heading off to the Stampede. I was fortunate enough to get a jacket and Chiori got wind pants. Helga picked up some fabric for a friend.

At the stampede we picked up tickets for the Grandstand show, then wandered through the Indian Village with its beautifully designed tepees. As we left the village, it began to rain - a storm that turned into a monsoon. We took refuge at a blacksmithing competition. We learned more about shoeing horses than we really wanted to know. We left there when it was time to go to the Grandstand show. Our seats were at least covered so we were spared the rain, but the temperature really dropped and we all were chilled. The chuckwagon races were interesting and the variety show was good - but long. We left shortly before the end as we were all cold and wet. However, we had a good view of the fireworks from the parking lot!

July 12/94

The whole tribe got up early so we could participate in one of the many free chuckwagon breakfasts - this one in southwest Calgary at the William Roper Hull facility where one of Carol's and Doug's nieces works. There was a lot of entertainment, including Indian dancers, a marching band, clowns, car display, various entertainers, and even a Brahma bull for photo ops. Chiori sat on the bull while Helga & I stood beside it.

On to the Stampede for the afternoon rodeo. I think this was a once-in-a-lifetime experience for all of us as we had our fill of bronc and bull riding. We did learn that a strap is placed around the hind quarters of the animal to make it buck.

Back to "camp" for a delicious dinner and to meet new "relatives" as Chris and Robin dropped in. The only thing to mar our fun times was the fact that Doug had had a biopsy on a lump in his breast that day. Since he felt fine, everyone was sure the results would be negative.

July 13/94

Time to bid farewell to Calgary and press on to Banff. The mountains never cease to astound me with their magnificence. We lunched at the Banff Springs Hotel and explored its grounds. Then we went to Sulphur Mountain gondola ride and looked down on Banff from the mountain top. Mountain goats were much in evidence. Following that we went to the Hot Springs for a dip. Helga and Chiori were a bit disappointed that the water was in a manmade pool, rather than on natural rocks. Chiori also told us that in Japan bathers went in to hot springs in the buff.

Elk were roaming the streets of Banff as we drove

by and began our journey along the Bow Valley Parkway to Lake Louise. We stopped along the way to admire the view and wildflowers.

Arriving in Lake Louise we were enthusiastically welcomed by Karen, Mark and Mason. After dinner Karen and Chiori went on a bike ride while the rest of us strolled along the banks of the Bow to the old Lake Louise station which has been converted into a lovely restaurant. Two railway cars have also been converted into dining rooms.

July 14/94

We drove to the Columbia Icefilds with several scenic stops along the way. Mark even found us at one. We took the Icefields tour in the specially constructed vehicles and learned quite a bit about glaciers. In the evening we crossed the border at Kicking Horse pass into B.C. so we could go to one of the highest and most scenic falls in Canada, Takakkaw Falls. Here, Mark and Mason were our tour guides. Back to Lake Louise to pick up Karen and go to The Station Restaurant for dinner.

July 15/94

Our last day in the Mountains. Karen and Mason accompanied us to Moraine Lake and the Valley of the Ten Peaks which we see on the back of our twenty dollar bills. We climbed the slate pile for a view. Next we all went to Lake Louise itself and the Chateau. Our time was limited so we walked nearly to the end of the lake and spent a short time in the Chateau shops. Then it was time to say goodbye to Karen and Mason and begin our trip back to Calgary so I could hop a plane to Vancouver. Much to my surprise, Doug and Carol were at the airport to say goodbye. What wonderful, thoughtful people!

Chiori and Helga went back to the "campground" where they had a steak dinner and met cousin John.

Next day they started their long drive back to Ontario.

EMERALD WATERS
OF THE ROCKIES

A collection of 64 fine, large format photographs featuring many aspects of water in the Canadian Rockies.

Life giving and nourishing, the water in the Canadian Rockies is still cool, clear and unpolluted. Breathtaking colors of water vary depending on contents and density of glacial silt, time of day and year. Spring and, especially, late summer brings the best, clearest water coloration. Early summer waters are muddy and silty due to snow and glacial run-off. The best time for water sports and fishing is the second half of the summer.

Viewing and photographing lakes and rivers is a year-round attraction. Every season has its own, different angle, challenge and pleasure.

Explore and admire the waters of the Rockies but leave them pristine and undisturbed for others to enjoy.

Glacier-fed Peyto Lake is surrounded by the jagged peaks of the Wapta Icefield and photographed from Observation Peak (3174 m.) Banff National Park.

Spectacular Hector Lake is located at the east end of the Wapta Icefield, the silt from which creates the emerald color of the water. Photographed from Mt. Hector (3394 m.) Banff National Park.

One of the many streams coming from the glaciated north side of Mt. Edith Cavell. Jasper National Park.

The cascading waters of Nigel Creek Falls, just northwest of the Columbia Icefield. Jasper National Park.

One of Canada's mighty rivers, the Fraser, near its source. Mount Robson Provincial Park.

The world renowned Banff Springs Hotel, adorned by a spectacular rainbow. Banff National Park.

Silty and muddy from the spring run-off, the water of Kicking Horse River and the Wapta Falls. Yoho National Park.

Canada Goose (Branta canadensis). Proud and vigilant parents with a record brood of twenty-nine goslings.

The great inhabitant of the wetlands, the majestic Moose (Alces alces) is the world's largest deer.

Hikers enjoy the peace and scenery around the Saskatchewan Glacier and the Columbia Icefield. Banff National Park.

A late autumn image of serene Pyramid Lake. Jasper National Park.

Mirror-like Honeymoon Lake and the Endless Chain Range. Jasper National Park.

Covered by low clouds, Banff townsite and surrounding mountains as viewed from the slopes of Mt. Norquay. Banff National Park.

The Kananaskis Lakes and Valley and the Opal Range photographed from Mt. Foch (3179 m.) one misty summer morning.

The pristine wilderness around Baker Lake, with the Sawback Range in the background. Banff National Park.

Left: Bow Lake, Falls and Glacier, and the peaks of the Wapta Icefield. Banff National Park.

The cascading water of Paradise Creek creates a spectacular waterfalls system called the Giant Steps. Paradise Valley, Banff National Park.

A peaceful early winter scene of the Third Vermilion Lake, just west of Banff townsite. Banff National Park.

The mystery of nocturnal Bow Lake and surrounding peaks - Mt. Hector (left), Bow Peak and Crowfoot Mountain. Banff National Park.

Left Upper: Tranquil Second Vermilion Lake and Mt. Rundle.

Left Lower: Grizzly bear (Ursus arctos) decides to "cool off" by taking a dip in Wapta Lake on a warm summer night. Yoho National Park.

Deep in the mountain wilderness, at the foot of Pharaoh Peak (2711 m.), Mummy Lake lies surrounded by timberline beauty. Banff National Park.

East Lyell Glacier is located west of the Howse River and Glacier Lake, and is the main water source of the Glacier River. Banff National Park.

Living up to its name, Emerald Lake is the shining emerald jewel of Yoho National Park. Photographed from the east slopes of Mt. Burgess.

Overlooking the west end of Lake Louise and surrounding mountains from the Little Beehive. Banff National Park.

Bronzed by the rising sun, Castle Mountain (2766 m.) dominates the wintry Bow River. Banff National Park.

A tranquil early winter scene of the Bow River, just west of Banff townsite. Banff National Park.

Engelmann spruce and golden larch forest around picturesque Elizabeth Lake. Mt. Assiniboine Provincial Park.

The cool, clear, green waters of Takumm Creek in the Prospector's Valley. Kootenay National Park.

The famous Peyto Lake and, located to the north, an unknown, unnamed green tarn. A rugged scene, dominated by the scree high country scape. Banff National Park.

West of Boulder Pass lies small but picturesque Hidden Lake. Fed by the meltwater from Mt. Richardson's Glacier, from whence the picture was taken. Banff National Park.

A glorious sunrise on Lake Magog. Dusted by the first autumn snow, is Mt. Assiniboine (3618 m.) on the left and Sunburst Peak (2804 m.) Mt. Assiniboine Provincial Park.

Left: The monarch of the Canadian Rockies, Mt. Robson is reflected in Robson River and stands 3954 meters above sea level. Mt. Robson Provincial Park.

A "bird's-eye view" of autumnish Lake Minnewanka, photographed from the summit of Cascade Mountain (2998 m.) Banff National Park.

Summer, winter or in-between, Lake Louise is a year round paradise and well worth admiring anytime. Banff National Park.

High up on the western slopes of Mt. Temple hangs a picturesque little jewel - Lake Annette, Paradise Valley. Banff National Park.

Small near its source, the Fraser River tumbles down over Overlander Falls. Mount Robson Provincial Park.

The confluence of the silt-laden Kicking Horse River and the clear, green Amiskwi River. Yoho National Park.

Originating from the Winkchemna Glacier, the cool, clear waters of Moraine Creek rush toward Moraine Lake. Banff National Park.

An impressive view unfolds from Fossil Mountain (2946 m.). On the left is Mt. Redoubt (2902 m.), with Redoubt Lake below. In the center nests Ptarmigan Lake. The trail on the right leads to Deception Pass and Skoki. Banff National Park.

West of Deception Pass on the slopes of Ptarmigan Peak and the Wall of Jericho, are located the Skoki Lakes. The upper lake is named Zigadenus, the lower, Myosotis. Photographed from Fossil Mountain (2946 m.) Banff National Park.

The clear life-giving waters of a mountain stream rush down the slopes of Mt. Hector. Banff National Park.

The humble, but pretty, dandelion (Taraxacum scopulorum) is ever present in the Rockies. This early spring harbinger provides valuable protein for many mammals, including just-out-of-hibernation bears.

Its striking color and spectacular surroundings make Peyto Lake one of the premier tourist attractions of the Rockies. Banff National Park.

A late autumn image of Moraine Lake and the surrounding peaks. Glaciated Mt. Fay (3234 m.) stands at the center. Banff National Park.

A glacier-fed blue jewel of Banff National Park - pristine and beautiful Peyto Lake.

Bow Glacier and Bow Lake, where the Bow River originates. Banff National Park.

A mirror-like oasis of tranquility, Upper Waterfowl Lake at sunrise. The area provides an excellent habitat for moose and waterfowl. Banff National Park.

A perfect reflection of Crowfoot Mountain (3063 m.) in Bow Lake on a perfect summer morning.
The fishing looks perfect, as does the weather. Banff National Park.

A familiar sign of autumn, when water is warmer than air - a morning mist over Patricia Lake near the town of Jasper. Jasper National Park.

Left: Canoeing, kayaking - paddling on the Kicking Horse River in Yoho National Park. The Ottertail Range is in the background.

Endless mountain vistas and pristine wilderness surround spectacular Maligne Lake. Jasper National Park.

The white-water rafting on Athabasca River, near Jasper, is an adventurous way to enjoy the scenery. Jasper National Park.

The glacier-fed Kinney Lake - accessible by comfortable Berg Lake Trail and photographed from the southwestern slopes of Mt. Robson. Mt. Robson Provincial Park.

Accessible by restricted road and hiking trails, Lake O'Hara is well known for its alpine beauty and rich flora and fauna. Yoho National Park.

Late autumn morning mist over picturesque Patricia Lake. Jasper National Park.

The harbingers of coming spring - Canada Goose (Branta canadensis) feeding on the Sunwapta River north of the Columbia Icefield. Jasper National Park.

It is hard to believe how clear water can be until one sees it in a mountain lake like Lower Consolation Lake. Banff National Park.

Right: Sailing the cool, clear waters of Edith Lake. Pyramid Mountain (2766 m.) is in the background. Jasper National Park.

White-water rafting on a wild and spectacular Maligne River (above and left). A wilderness adventure to remember for a lifetime. Jasper National Park abounds in wildlife, rich flora and fine mountain scenery, with plenty of space for all.

The Author's Environmental Message

There was a beautiful, pristine wilderness thriving in the Canadian Rockies - flourishing for millions of years. Flora and fauna complemented each other, providing a sustainable environment for all. Due to changes of climate, some forms of life came and went, but life continued more or less undisturbed until...a new species arrived on the scene.

At the beginning, Homo Sapiens (a hunter and gatherer), behaved like the other animals - blending harmoniously into the environment.

Gradually, however, humans became a very dominant species and began to change the environment to suit their needs and liking. In a very short time humanity went from stick, bow, shovel and pick to bulldozers that can level several square kilometers in a single day.

Open pit mining and clear cut logging began and continue to this day, threatening to upset the planet's ecological balance. The noble and considerate people who try to protect the environment and stop the destruction, are thrown in jail like common criminals. Is this democracy in action?

We are told we "must" produce, consume, grow. If our Gross National Product grows only 2 - 3% per year, we should consider it a disaster. We "need" more and more.

We should realize that each new gadget and knick-knack we buy required raw materials and energy to produce it (and it will, most likely wind up in a garbage dump in a short time). More production and consumption means more pollution and damage to the environment.

Disposable and/or overly packaged products must be rejected. Do not buy them.

Do we really "need" two cars, two homes, two TV's, two boats and so on? Have you ever thought about where all the garbage and waste we produce goes?

It goes exactly nowhere! It stays here with us, permanently damaging the environment - the very air we breathe, the water we drink and the food we eat.

There are too many of us, concentrated in too many small areas.

Would you like to live in a penguin colony? How about in Hong Kong, where the population density is 9000 people per square mile?

Right now, we are eating up all the fish of the seas. Perhaps we start to reduce our population before we become desperate enough to eat each other.

This small planet of ours cannot continue to support billions of people in comfort. Green lands shrink in direct proportion to the population explosion.

Where are you rushing, Homo Sapiens? To your own funeral?

George Brybycin is a mountain man, naturalist, photographer and publisher who spends most of his life exploring, admiring and learning from nature.

The Canadian Rockies are his year-round home and playground.

As the world rushes to accumulate an excess of produced goods, George goes in exactly the opposite direction. He embraces noble ideas, humanity and a vision of the future. Above all, he worries about the environment. And for good reason.

Is there much hope, George asks, considering that everywhere, so much seems to go wrong. Of course there is hope.

If wisdom, goodwill and positive intentions prevail, together we can move mountains.

To begin with, you could find space on your property to plant two, five or ten trees. Buy a plastic Christmas tree and use it twenty or thirty times - you will save that many real trees (if everyone did this, it could save millions of trees every year).

Recycle everything you can, and buy only environment friendly products.

It is getting to the point that not only our health, but our very lives depend on maintaining a clean, healthy environment.